Edge AI: The Future of Intelligent Computing at the Device Level

Introduction

E dge AI is revolutionizing the way artificial intelligence is deployed, enabling real-time processing and decision-making directly on edge devices. By minimizing reliance on cloud infrastructure, Edge AI enhances speed, efficiency, security, and autonomy across various industries. This guide explores the fundamentals, benefits, applications, and best practices for implementing Edge AI solutions effectively.

What is Edge AI?

Edge AI refers to the deployment of artificial intelligence models on edge devices such as IoT sensors, smartphones, drones, and embedded systems. Unlike traditional AI, which relies on cloud computing, Edge AI processes data locally on the device, reducing latency and improving performance.

Why Edge AI Matters

With the increasing demand for real-time AI applications, Edge AI offers several advantages:

- **Low Latency**: Immediate processing without waiting for cloud response.
- **Enhanced Privacy & Security**: Data remains on the device, reducing exposure to cyber threats.
- **Reduced Bandwidth Usage**: Lower dependency on network connectivity and cloud storage.
- **Energy Efficiency**: Optimized computations for battery-powered and resource-constrained devices.
- **Operational Autonomy**: Enables AI-driven decision-making even in remote or offline environments.

Who Should Read This Guide?

This guide is designed for:

- **AI Engineers & Developers**: Seeking to optimize AI models for edge deployment.
- **IoT & Embedded System Developers**: Integrating AI into smart devices and industrial applications.
- **Data Scientists & ML Engineers**: Adapting AI models for decentralized computing.
- **Business & Technology Leaders**: Understanding Edge AI's impact on digital transformation and innovation.

What You Will Learn

Throughout this guide, we will cover:

1. **Fundamentals of Edge AI**: Architecture, key components, and deployment strategies.
2. **Hardware & Software Ecosystem**: Choosing the right tools and frameworks for Edge AI.

3. **Optimizing AI Models for the Edge**: Techniques for model compression, quantization, and inference acceleration.

4. **Security & Privacy Considerations**: Ensuring safe and reliable AI applications.

5. **Industry Applications & Case Studies**: Real-world implementations across healthcare, automotive, manufacturing, and more.

6. **Best Practices & Future Trends**: Maximizing performance and staying ahead in the evolving Edge AI landscape.

This book provides a structured and engaging journey into Edge AI, equipping professionals with the knowledge and skills needed to harness the power of AI at the edge. Let's get started!

Chapter 1: Understanding Edge AI

Definition of Edge AI

Edge AI refers to the deployment of artificial intelligence (AI) models directly on edge devices, enabling them to process data locally rather than relying on centralized cloud computing. These edge devices include smartphones, IoT sensors, cameras, drones, autonomous vehicles, and industrial robots. Unlike traditional AI systems that depend on powerful cloud servers, Edge AI operates with limited computational resources while maintaining efficiency and responsiveness.

At its core, Edge AI integrates machine learning (ML) models with edge computing, allowing real-time data processing, decision-making, and automation at the source of data generation. By reducing dependency on cloud infrastructure, Edge AI enhances speed, security, and reliability in AI-powered applications.

How Edge AI Differs from Cloud AI

Cloud AI and Edge AI represent two different paradigms in artificial intelligence deployment. While both leverage machine learning and deep learning algorithms, their fundamental difference lies in where the computation occurs.

1. **Processing Location:**
   - **Cloud AI:** Data is sent to centralized cloud servers for processing and inference.
   - **Edge AI:** Data is processed locally on the device, reducing latency and bandwidth usage.

2. **Latency:**
   - **Cloud AI:** Higher latency due to the time required to transmit data to the cloud and back.
   - **Edge AI:** Low latency as processing happens near the source.

3. **Bandwidth Consumption:**
   - **Cloud AI:** Requires constant internet connectivity and large data transmission.

- Edge AI: Reduces data transfer requirements, saving bandwidth costs.

4. **Security and Privacy:**
   - **Cloud AI:** Data must be sent to external servers, increasing exposure to cyber threats.
   - **Edge AI:** Keeps sensitive data on local devices, improving privacy and security.

5. **Reliability:**
   - **Cloud AI:** Dependent on network connectivity; service disruptions affect functionality.
   - **Edge AI:** Can function independently even without an internet connection.

Advantages and Challenges of Edge AI

Advantages

1. **Real-Time Processing:** Immediate decision-making capabilities, crucial for applications like autonomous driving and industrial automation.

2. **Reduced Latency:** Faster responses as data is processed locally, making it ideal for time-sensitive tasks.

3. **Lower Bandwidth Usage:** Reduces the need for constant data transmission, optimizing network efficiency.

4. **Enhanced Security & Privacy:** Sensitive data remains on the device, reducing exposure to cybersecurity threats.

5. **Operational Reliability:** Works without relying on cloud connectivity, ensuring continued performance in remote or unstable network conditions.

6. **Energy Efficiency:** Optimized AI models require lower power consumption, making Edge AI suitable for battery-operated devices.

Challenges

1. **Limited Computing Power:** Edge devices often have constrained processing capabilities compared to cloud servers.

2. **Storage Constraints:** AI models need to be lightweight to fit within device memory.

3. **Complex Deployment & Maintenance:** Updates and maintenance require distributed strategies across multiple edge devices.
4. **Scalability Issues:** Deploying AI across thousands of devices demands robust management frameworks.
5. **Model Optimization Requirements:** AI models must be compressed and optimized to run efficiently on edge hardware.

Key Industries Benefiting from Edge AI

1. Healthcare

Edge AI enables real-time diagnostics and monitoring through wearable devices, smart sensors, and medical imaging tools. It helps detect early signs of diseases, automate patient monitoring, and enhance telemedicine applications.

2. Manufacturing & Industrial Automation

Factories leverage Edge AI for predictive maintenance, quality control, and automation of assembly lines. AI-powered sensors detect equipment failures before they occur, reducing downtime and improving productivity.

3. Autonomous Vehicles & Transportation

Self-driving cars and smart transportation systems use Edge AI for real-time navigation, object detection, and collision avoidance. By processing data locally, vehicles respond faster to road conditions and obstacles.

4. Retail & Smart Commerce

Edge AI powers cashier-less stores, real-time customer analytics, and personalized shopping experiences. AI cameras analyze shopper behavior, optimize inventory, and detect fraudulent activities.

5. Agriculture

Smart farming uses Edge AI to monitor soil conditions, detect plant diseases, and optimize irrigation systems.

Drones equipped with AI analyze crop health and automate pesticide spraying.

6. Smart Cities & IoT

Edge AI enhances urban infrastructure with intelligent traffic management, smart surveillance, and efficient energy consumption. AI-driven security cameras identify threats in real-time without relying on cloud servers.

7. Telecommunications & 5G

Edge AI optimizes network performance, reduces latency in 5G applications, and enhances mobile computing experiences.

8. Defense & Security

Military and law enforcement agencies use Edge AI for real-time surveillance, facial recognition, and threat detection in high-risk areas.

9. Energy & Utilities

Smart grids and power management systems rely on Edge AI for real-time monitoring, demand forecasting, and energy efficiency improvements.

Conclusion

Edge AI is revolutionizing industries by enabling real-time, secure, and efficient AI applications. While it presents certain challenges, its advantages make it a crucial technology for the future of AI-driven automation and intelligence. As Edge AI continues to evolve, advancements in hardware and model optimization will further expand its potential across diverse sectors.

Chapter 2: Edge AI Hardware

Edge AI relies on specialized hardware to process machine learning models efficiently at the edge of the network, reducing dependency on cloud computing. This chapter explores key hardware components that make Edge AI possible.

AI Chips and Accelerators

1. NVIDIA Jetson

NVIDIA Jetson is a leading platform for AI at the edge, featuring powerful GPUs optimized for deep learning and computer vision.

- **Jetson Nano:** Budget-friendly option for lightweight AI models.
- **Jetson Xavier NX:** Offers higher performance for robotics and autonomous systems.
- **Jetson AGX Orin:** High-end solution for industrial and automotive AI applications.

2. Google Coral

Google Coral is designed for fast inferencing with low power consumption. It integrates Tensor Processing Units (TPUs) optimized for running TensorFlow Lite models.

- **Coral Dev Board:** Compact development board with a built-in Edge TPU.
- **Coral USB Accelerator:** External TPU for existing edge devices.

3. Intel Movidius

Intel's Movidius Vision Processing Units (VPUs) enable efficient deep learning inference with minimal power consumption.

- **Myriad X:** Supports neural network acceleration and computer vision workloads.
- **Neural Compute Stick 2 (NCS2):** USB device for AI prototyping on edge devices.

Edge AI Computing Devices

1. Raspberry Pi

Raspberry Pi is a popular single-board computer used for Edge AI projects.

- **Raspberry Pi 4 & 5:** Supports AI inferencing with additional accelerators like Coral TPU or Intel NCS2.
- **Raspberry Pi Compute Module 4 (CM4):** Designed for industrial AI applications.

2. Arduino

While Arduino is primarily used for microcontroller-based projects, it supports AI applications with external accelerators.

- **Arduino Portenta H7:** Features a dual-core Cortex-M7 processor for AI workloads.
- **Arduino Nicla Vision:** Combines AI processing with image recognition capabilities.

3. TPUs (Tensor Processing Units)

TPUs are specialized processors optimized for machine learning inference.

- **Edge TPU by Google:** Runs TensorFlow Lite models efficiently.
- **Cloud TPU:** Designed for high-performance AI workloads but less relevant for edge applications.

4. FPGAs (Field Programmable Gate Arrays)

FPGAs provide a reconfigurable hardware solution for AI inference with low latency.

- **Xilinx Kria & Alveo:** Used for industrial AI and edge computing.
- **Intel Stratix & Cyclone FPGAs:** Support real-time AI processing.

IoT and Embedded Systems for Edge AI

Edge AI is closely integrated with **IoT and embedded systems**, enabling real-time data processing on smart devices.

Key Applications:

- **Smart cameras** (security, facial recognition, surveillance)
- **Autonomous drones** (real-time navigation, object detection)
- **Industrial automation** (predictive maintenance, quality control)
- **Smart healthcare devices** (wearable health monitoring)

Challenges in Edge AI Hardware:

- **Power efficiency:** Limited battery life and thermal management.
- **Computational constraints:** Need for optimized models due to hardware limitations.
- **Security risks:** Edge AI devices require robust cybersecurity measures.

Chapter 3: Edge AI Software and Frameworks

Edge AI software plays a crucial role in optimizing machine learning models for deployment on low-power devices. Unlike cloud-based AI, edge AI models must be lightweight, efficient, and capable of real-time inference. This chapter explores the most widely used frameworks and tools that enable AI at the edge.

3.1 TensorFlow Lite

TensorFlow Lite (TFLite) is a lightweight version of TensorFlow designed for mobile and edge devices. It optimizes deep learning models for fast and efficient inference with minimal resource consumption.

Key Features:

✓ Model quantization for reduced size and improved performance.

✓ Hardware acceleration support (GPU, Edge TPU, NNAPI, XNNPACK).

✓ Pre-trained models for common tasks like image classification and object detection.

Workflow:

1. **Train a model** in TensorFlow.
2. **Convert the model** to TensorFlow Lite format (.tflite).
3. **Optimize** using quantization or pruning.
4. **Deploy on an edge device** (e.g., Raspberry Pi, Jetson Nano, Android).

Use Cases:

- Real-time image classification on mobile phones.
- Object detection on smart cameras.
- Speech recognition on embedded AI assistants.

3.2 ONNX Runtime

Open Neural Network Exchange (ONNX) Runtime is a cross-platform framework that allows models trained in different frameworks (TensorFlow, PyTorch, Scikit-learn) to run efficiently on edge hardware.

Key Features:

✓ Supports multiple AI frameworks via ONNX format.
✓ Hardware acceleration with NVIDIA TensorRT, DirectML, and OpenVINO.
✓ Optimized for low-latency inference on CPUs, GPUs, and custom accelerators.

Workflow:

1. **Train a model** in TensorFlow or PyTorch.
2. **Convert it to ONNX format** using torch.onnx.export() or tf2onnx.
3. **Optimize the model** using ONNX Runtime optimizations.
4. **Deploy** on edge devices, including Windows, Linux, and embedded platforms.

Use Cases:

- AI-powered medical imaging analysis.
- Edge-based fraud detection systems.
- Industrial automation with low-latency AI inference.

3.3 OpenVINO

OpenVINO (Open Visual Inference and Neural network Optimization) is Intel's toolkit for accelerating deep learning models on Intel hardware, including CPUs, VPUs, and FPGAs.

Key Features:

✓ Supports TensorFlow, PyTorch, and ONNX models.

✓ Optimized for Intel processors, including Movidius VPUs and Intel GPUs.

✓ Low-latency AI inference with model optimization and quantization.

Workflow:

1. **Train a model** in TensorFlow or PyTorch.
2. **Convert it to OpenVINO format** using the Model Optimizer.
3. **Optimize for Intel hardware** with OpenVINO's runtime.
4. **Deploy on Intel-based edge devices** for fast inference.

Use Cases:

- AI-powered video analytics for smart surveillance.
- Edge-based speech processing in voice assistants.
- AI-driven defect detection in manufacturing.

3.4 PyTorch Mobile

PyTorch Mobile is an extension of PyTorch that enables deep learning model deployment on mobile and embedded devices.

Key Features:

✓ Supports both Android and iOS deployment.

✓ Uses TorchScript for model conversion and execution.

✓ Allows on-device training and inference.

Workflow:

1. **Train a PyTorch model** on a desktop/server.
2. **Convert to TorchScript format** using torch.jit.trace().
3. **Deploy on mobile** using PyTorch Mobile APIs.

Use Cases:

- Real-time AI-driven augmented reality (AR) applications.
- Mobile-based speech recognition and translation.
- AI-powered medical diagnostics on handheld devices.

3.5 TinyML: Ultra-Low-Power AI for Edge Devices

TinyML is a specialized branch of machine learning focused on running AI models on ultra-low-power microcontrollers and embedded systems.

Key Features:

✓ Runs on microcontrollers with limited RAM (e.g., ARM Cortex-M).

✓ Optimized for energy efficiency (operates on batteries for months/years).

✓ Uses model compression and quantization to reduce size.

Popular TinyML Frameworks:

- **TensorFlow Lite for Microcontrollers (TFLM):** Runs on devices with as little as 16 KB RAM.
- **Edge Impulse:** A platform for building and deploying TinyML models.
- **uTensor:** An embedded AI framework for ARM Cortex-M devices.

Workflow:

1. **Train a lightweight model** on a standard machine.
2. **Convert it into an optimized format** (TFLite, uTensor, etc.).
3. **Deploy on microcontrollers** like Arduino, ESP32, or STM32.

Use Cases:

- AI-powered smart sensors in IoT networks.
- Low-power predictive maintenance systems.
- Wearable health monitoring devices.

Conclusion

Edge AI software frameworks enable efficient model deployment on resource-constrained devices. Choosing the right framework depends on hardware compatibility, performance requirements, and energy constraints.

Framework	Best For	Hardware Support
TensorFlow Lite	Mobile, IoT, and embedded AI	Android, Raspberry Pi, Edge TPU, ARM CPUs
ONNX Runtime	Cross-platform AI inference	NVIDIA, Intel, Windows, Linux
OpenVINO	Intel-optimized AI models	Intel CPUs, VPUs, FPGAs
PyTorch Mobile	AI deployment on mobile devices	Android, iOS
TinyML	AI on microcontrollers	Arduino, ESP32, STM32

Understanding and leveraging these frameworks is essential for building **fast, efficient, and scalable Edge AI applications**.

Chapter 4: Benefits of Edge AI

Edge AI is transforming industries by enabling **real-time intelligence** directly on devices without relying on cloud computing. This shift provides numerous advantages, including lower latency, enhanced security, cost efficiency, and scalability. This chapter explores the key benefits of Edge AI and why it is becoming a game-changer for AI-driven applications.

4.1 Low Latency and Real-Time Decision-Making

One of the most significant advantages of Edge AI is its ability to **process data locally**, reducing the time required for decision-making. Traditional AI systems often rely on cloud computing, which introduces latency due to data transmission over the internet. In contrast, Edge AI enables instant processing on-site, making it ideal for applications requiring **real-time responsiveness**.

Key Benefits:

✓ **Immediate response times** (milliseconds instead of seconds).

✓ **Reliable performance** even with unstable or limited internet connections.

✓ **Critical for time-sensitive applications** like autonomous vehicles, robotics, and industrial automation.

Use Cases:

- **Autonomous vehicles:** Detect obstacles and make driving decisions in real time.
- **Industrial automation:** Identify defects in manufacturing lines instantly.
- **Smart cameras:** Perform facial recognition and anomaly detection without cloud delays.

☐ **Example:** A self-driving car cannot afford a delay when identifying pedestrians. Edge AI processes sensor data locally, enabling split-second decisions that **enhance safety**.

4.2 Enhanced Privacy and Security

In traditional cloud-based AI, sensitive data must be transmitted to remote servers for processing. This **introduces risks** such as data breaches, unauthorized access, and compliance issues. Edge AI **keeps data local**, significantly reducing exposure to cyber threats.

Key Benefits:

✓ **Minimizes data transmission risks**, reducing exposure to hackers.

✓ **Complies with data protection regulations** like GDPR and HIPAA.

✓ **Improves user privacy** by processing personal data on the device itself.

Use Cases:

- **Healthcare AI:** Patient data remains on the device, ensuring privacy.
- **Surveillance systems:** AI-powered cameras analyze footage locally, reducing the risk of cyberattacks.
- **IoT security:** Devices can detect and respond to cybersecurity threats without cloud intervention.

☐ **Example:** A hospital using Edge AI-powered wearables can **analyze patient vitals on-site**, eliminating the need to send personal health data to external cloud servers.

4.3 Reduced Cloud Dependency and Lower Costs

Running AI workloads in the cloud can be expensive due to data storage, bandwidth, and computational resources. Edge AI **reduces cloud dependency**, leading to substantial cost savings.

Key Benefits:

✓ **Minimizes cloud storage and processing costs.**

✓ **Reduces bandwidth usage** by processing data locally.

✓ **Ensures functionality even in offline environments.**

Use Cases:

- **Retail analytics:** AI-driven insights generated on-site, reducing cloud processing costs.
- **Smart agriculture:** Edge AI monitors soil conditions and crop health without needing continuous cloud connectivity.
- **Autonomous drones:** Process flight data and navigation locally, saving bandwidth and cloud costs.

☐ **Example:** A smart factory using Edge AI reduces expenses by **analyzing sensor data locally** instead of constantly uploading terabytes of data to the cloud.

4.4 Scalability and Energy Efficiency

Edge AI enables businesses to scale AI-driven applications efficiently by distributing intelligence across multiple edge devices rather than relying on **centralized cloud resources**. Additionally, edge computing is more energy-efficient since it reduces the need for high-power cloud data centers.

Key Benefits:

✓ **Scales efficiently** without requiring extensive cloud infrastructure.

✓ **Reduces power consumption**, making it ideal for battery-powered devices.

✓ **Works seamlessly in remote locations** with limited internet access.

Use Cases:

- **Smart grids:** Optimize energy distribution based on real-time power demand.

- **Wearable AI:** Runs AI models efficiently on low-power devices.
- **Edge-based robotics:** AI-powered robots perform tasks without excessive energy consumption.

☐ **Example:** A fleet of smart surveillance drones using Edge AI can **process video footage onboard**, eliminating the need for continuous data transmission to cloud servers and **extending battery life**.

Conclusion

Edge AI offers **unmatched advantages** by bringing AI processing closer to the source of data. Its **low latency, privacy protection, cost efficiency, and scalability** make it the ideal choice for **next-generation AI applications**.

Benefit	Advantage	Example Use Case
Low Latency	Real-time AI decision-making	Autonomous vehicles, industrial automation
Enhanced Security	Local processing protects sensitive data	Healthcare, surveillance, IoT security
Cost Efficiency	Reduces cloud processing and storage costs	Smart factories, retail analytics
Energy Efficiency	Optimized power consumption for edge devices	Wearables, drones, smart grids

With these benefits, Edge AI is set to revolutionize industries by **making AI more accessible, responsive, and efficient** in real-world applications.

Chapter 5: Use Cases of Edge AI

Edge AI is revolutionizing multiple industries by enabling real-time decision-making, reducing reliance on cloud computing, and improving efficiency. This chapter explores key applications where Edge AI is making a significant impact, from **smart surveillance** to **autonomous vehicles** and **healthcare**.

5.1 Smart Surveillance and Security

Security systems are evolving from passive monitoring to **AI-powered smart surveillance** that can detect threats in real time. By processing video feeds locally, Edge AI reduces bandwidth usage and improves response times.

Key Benefits:

✓ **Real-time threat detection** (e.g., recognizing suspicious activity).

✓ **Privacy protection** (video is processed on-site, reducing cloud exposure).

✓ **Reduced storage and network costs** (processes only relevant data).

Use Cases:

- **AI-powered CCTV cameras** can detect unauthorized access and trigger alerts.
- **Facial recognition systems** for access control in secure locations.
- **License plate recognition** for smart parking and law enforcement.

☐ **Example:** A smart city uses **Edge AI surveillance cameras** that detect unusual behavior (e.g., unattended bags in a public space) and notify authorities in real time.

5.2 Autonomous Vehicles and Drones

Self-driving cars and autonomous drones rely on **Edge AI** to process vast amounts of sensor data in real time. Sending this data to the cloud would cause **dangerous delays**, making local AI processing essential.

Key Benefits:

✓ **Instant decision-making** for navigation and obstacle avoidance.

✓ **Reduced reliance on cloud connectivity**, improving reliability.

✓ **Increased safety** through continuous AI-powered monitoring.

Use Cases:

- **Self-driving cars** analyze road conditions and make split-second driving decisions.
- **Delivery drones** navigate through cities using AI-powered object detection.

- **Autonomous farm vehicles** optimize crop planting and harvesting.

☐ **Example:** Tesla's **Autopilot system** uses Edge AI to process camera and radar data in real time, allowing the car to **react instantly** to traffic conditions.

5.3 Healthcare and Medical Devices

Edge AI is transforming healthcare by enabling **real-time patient monitoring**, diagnostics, and AI-assisted decision-making **without relying on cloud servers**.

Key Benefits:

✓ **Faster diagnosis** with on-device AI analysis.
✓ **Enhanced privacy** (patient data stays on the device).
✓ **Works in remote areas** without continuous internet access.

Use Cases:

- **AI-powered wearables** monitor heart rate, oxygen levels, and ECG in real time.
- **Smart ultrasound machines** use Edge AI for instant image analysis.
- **Remote patient monitoring systems** detect early signs of health issues.

□ **Example:** An Edge AI-powered **portable ECG monitor** can detect abnormal heart rhythms and alert doctors **instantly**, preventing heart attacks in high-risk patients.

5.4 Industrial Automation and Predictive Maintenance

Factories and industrial plants are adopting **Edge AI** to monitor equipment in real time, reducing **downtime** and improving **efficiency** through predictive maintenance.

Key Benefits:

✓ **Prevents unexpected failures** by detecting early signs of wear and tear.

✓ **Reduces operational costs** by optimizing machine performance.

✓ **Minimizes downtime** through proactive maintenance scheduling.

Use Cases:

- **AI-powered sensors** detect vibrations and temperature anomalies in machinery.
- **Edge AI robotics** optimize assembly line operations.
- **AI-driven quality control** detects defective products instantly.

☐ **Example:** A manufacturing plant uses **Edge AI sensors** to monitor motor vibrations and **predict failures before they happen**, saving thousands in maintenance costs.

5.5 Smart Cities and Environmental Monitoring

Smart cities leverage **Edge AI** to optimize traffic flow, monitor air quality, and enhance public services **in real time**.

Key Benefits:

✓ **Reduces traffic congestion** through AI-powered traffic signals.

✓ **Monitors air and water quality** in real time for pollution control.

✓ **Improves public safety** with AI-driven incident detection.

Use Cases:

- **Smart traffic lights** adjust in real time based on vehicle flow.
- **Edge AI environmental sensors** detect pollution levels and predict weather conditions.
- **AI-powered streetlights** adjust brightness based on pedestrian movement.

☐ **Example:** A **smart city project in Singapore** uses AI-powered traffic lights that adapt **dynamically** to reduce congestion and **improve commute times**.

5.6 Retail and Customer Experience Enhancement

Retailers use **Edge AI** to enhance **customer experiences**, **optimize inventory**, and improve **security**.

Key Benefits:

√ **Personalized shopping experiences** through AI-driven recommendations.

√ **Automated checkout systems** reduce wait times.

√ **Smart inventory tracking** minimizes losses and stock shortages.

Use Cases:

- **AI-powered cameras** analyze customer behavior to optimize store layout.
- **Smart shelves** track inventory in real time and notify restocking needs.
- **Cashierless stores** (e.g., Amazon Go) use Edge AI for seamless transactions.

☐ **Example:** Amazon Go stores use **Edge AI-powered cameras** and sensors to track items picked by customers, enabling **a completely checkout-free shopping experience**.

Conclusion

Edge AI is revolutionizing multiple industries by **bringing intelligence closer to the data source**, reducing latency, improving security, and **enabling real-time decision-making**.

Use Case	Advantage	Example
Smart Surveillance	Real-time threat detection	AI-powered CCTV cameras
Autonomous Vehicles & Drones	Instant navigation & obstacle avoidance	Tesla Autopilot, delivery drones
Healthcare & Medical Devices	On-device AI diagnostics & privacy protection	AI-powered ECG monitors
Industrial Automation	Predictive maintenance & efficiency	Edge AI sensors in factories
Smart Cities & Environmental AI	Traffic optimization & pollution monitoring	AI-powered traffic lights in smart cities
Retail & Customer Experience	Personalized shopping & automated checkout	Amazon Go cashierless stores

Edge AI is **shaping the future** by making AI **faster, smarter, and more accessible** across multiple domains. 🚀

Chapter 6: Implementing Edge AI Solutions

Implementing **Edge AI** involves multiple stages, from **data collection** to **model training**, **deployment**, and **continuous monitoring**. Unlike traditional cloud-based AI, Edge AI models must be **optimized for low-power, high-efficiency environments** while maintaining accuracy and performance.

This chapter provides a **step-by-step guide** to building and deploying Edge AI models, covering best practices and key considerations.

6.1 Steps to Develop an Edge AI Model

Developing an Edge AI solution follows a structured process:

Step 1: Define the Use Case and Requirements

✓ Identify the specific problem the Edge AI model will solve.

✓ Determine the **hardware constraints** (e.g., Raspberry Pi, NVIDIA Jetson, Google Coral).

✓ Define performance metrics (**accuracy, latency, power consumption**).

Step 2: Collect and Preprocess Data

✓ Gather high-quality datasets relevant to the problem.

✓ Clean, normalize, and annotate the data.

✓ Reduce the dataset size if necessary to fit edge constraints.

Step 3: Train and Optimize the Model

✓ Select a lightweight AI model suitable for Edge AI (**MobileNet, YOLO Tiny, TinyBERT, etc.**).

✓ Optimize the model using techniques like **quantization and pruning**.

✓ Test the model on edge hardware to measure **performance and power efficiency**.

Step 4: Deploy the Model to Edge Devices

✓ Convert the trained model to an **edge-compatible format** (TensorFlow Lite, ONNX, OpenVINO).

✓ Integrate with **hardware accelerators** (TPUs, FPGAs, GPUs).

✓ Use **containerization** (Docker, Kubernetes) for scalable deployment.

Step 5: Monitor and Update the Model

✓ Implement **on-device logging** to track model performance.

✓ Periodically **update and retrain** the model based on new data.

✓ Enable **remote model updates** to improve accuracy over time.

6.2 Data Collection and Preprocessing

High-quality data is **essential** for accurate Edge AI models. However, data collection at the edge comes with unique challenges, such as **limited storage and computing power**.

Best Practices for Edge AI Data Collection:

✓ **Use on-device data collection** to reduce cloud dependence.

✓ **Filter unnecessary data** to avoid excessive processing.

✓ **Ensure diverse datasets** to improve model generalization.

Preprocessing Techniques for Edge AI:

✓ **Data Normalization:** Standardize inputs for consistency.

✓ **Feature Extraction:** Reduce dimensionality while keeping important information.

✓ **Data Augmentation:** Generate more samples to improve model robustness.

✓ **Compression Techniques:** Reduce dataset size to fit edge constraints.

☐ **Example:** An Edge AI-powered **smart camera** only captures images when motion is detected, reducing unnecessary data collection and processing.

6.3 Model Training and Optimization for Edge Devices

Edge AI models must be **lightweight**, **fast**, and **energy-efficient** while maintaining high accuracy.

Choosing the Right Model Architecture

- **Lightweight CNNs** (e.g., MobileNet, TinyYOLO) for image processing.
- **Efficient Transformers** (e.g., TinyBERT, DistilBERT) for NLP tasks.
- **Quantized RNNs** for low-power speech recognition.

Optimization Techniques for Edge AI Models

✓ **Quantization:** Converts high-precision (FP32) models into low-precision (INT8) models for faster execution.

✓ **Pruning:** Removes less important neurons to **reduce model size** without affecting accuracy.

✓ **Knowledge Distillation:** Trains a smaller "student" model to mimic a larger "teacher" model.

✓ **Hardware Acceleration:** Uses TPUs, GPUs, or FPGAs to speed up inference.

☐ **Example:** Google Coral's Edge TPU **runs quantized models up to 4x faster** than a standard CPU, making it ideal for real-time AI applications.

6.4 Deployment Strategies for Edge AI

Deploying an Edge AI model requires careful consideration of **hardware compatibility, latency, and connectivity**.

Deployment Methods:

- **On-Device Inference:** Runs the model directly on an edge device (e.g., Raspberry Pi, Jetson Nano).
- **Edge Gateway Deployment:** Uses a **local edge server** to process AI models and send results to devices.
- **Hybrid Edge-Cloud:** Processes critical tasks at the edge while offloading complex computations to the cloud.

Key Considerations for Edge AI Deployment:

✓ **Model Format Compatibility:** Convert models to **TensorFlow Lite, OpenVINO, or ONNX**.

✓ **Latency and Performance:** Ensure the model runs within acceptable response times.

✓ **Security:** Implement **encryption** and **access control** for sensitive data.

☐ **Example:** A **smart factory** deploys an Edge AI-based predictive maintenance system that **detects machine failures on-site** while sending summarized data to the cloud for long-term analysis.

6.5 Continuous Monitoring and Updates

AI models **degrade over time** due to changes in the environment, new data patterns, and edge hardware wear. Continuous monitoring ensures the model remains **accurate and efficient**.

Key Aspects of Edge AI Model Monitoring:

✓ **Performance Logging:** Track **accuracy, inference time, and energy consumption**.
✓ **Error Detection:** Identify **misclassifications or unusual outputs**.
✓ **Remote Updates:** Enable **over-the-air (OTA) updates** for continuous improvement.

Retraining and Updating Edge AI Models:

1. **Collect real-world edge data** to detect performance drift.
2. **Retrain the model** on updated datasets using cloud or edge resources.

3. **Deploy the improved model** without disrupting edge operations.

□ **Example:** An AI-powered **wildlife monitoring system** updates its model periodically to recognize **new animal species** detected by Edge AI cameras.

Conclusion

Implementing Edge AI requires a structured approach, from **data collection** to **training, deployment, and monitoring**. Optimizing models for **low-power edge devices** ensures efficiency while **maintaining high performance**.

Stage	Key Considerations	Example
Data Collection & Preprocessing	Optimize for edge constraints, ensure data quality	Motion-triggered smart cameras
Model Training & Optimization	Use lightweight models, apply quantization & pruning	MobileNet on Raspberry Pi

Deployment Strategies	Choose on-device, edge gateway, or hybrid approach	AI-powered predictive maintenance in factories
Continuous Monitoring	Track performance, update models remotely	Smart surveillance adapting to new threats

By following these best practices, Edge AI solutions can be **efficient, scalable, and adaptable**, driving innovation across various industries.

Chapter 7: Challenges and Future of Edge AI

Edge AI is transforming industries by enabling **real-time, low-latency** decision-making without relying on cloud computing. However, deploying AI on edge devices comes with significant challenges, including **power constraints, interoperability issues, and ethical concerns**.

This chapter explores the **key challenges of Edge AI** and provides insights into the **future of AI on edge devices**.

7.1 Power and Resource Constraints

One of the biggest challenges in Edge AI is the **limited computational resources** available on edge devices. Unlike cloud-based AI, edge systems operate on **low-power processors, microcontrollers, and embedded hardware**, making it difficult to run complex AI models.

Challenges:

Limited Processing Power: Many edge devices rely on CPUs, microcontrollers, or low-power GPUs, which struggle with large AI models.

Energy Constraints: Running AI models continuously

on battery-powered devices (e.g., drones, wearables) drains power quickly.

Memory Limitations: Edge devices often have **small RAM and storage**, making it difficult to load large datasets and models.

Solutions:

- **Model Compression:** Use techniques like **quantization and pruning** to reduce model size without losing accuracy.
- **Efficient AI Architectures:** Deploy **lightweight models** like MobileNet, TinyYOLO, or DistilBERT.
- **Edge Accelerators:** Use **AI chips (e.g., Google Coral, NVIDIA Jetson, Intel Movidius)** to offload AI computations.
- **Low-Power AI Algorithms:** Implement energy-efficient neural networks designed for edge devices.

☐ **Example:** Smart security cameras use **motion-triggered AI** instead of continuously analyzing video, reducing power consumption.

7.2 Standardization and Interoperability Issues

The Edge AI ecosystem is fragmented, with **different hardware vendors, software frameworks, and AI models**. This lack of standardization makes it difficult to develop cross-platform AI solutions.

Challenges:

Incompatible AI Frameworks: AI models trained in TensorFlow, PyTorch, or ONNX may not always work seamlessly across different edge devices.

Communication Protocols: Edge devices use different connectivity standards (Wi-Fi, 5G, LoRa, Zigbee), complicating integration.

Diverse Hardware Architectures: AI accelerators (TPUs, GPUs, FPGAs) require specific software optimizations.

Solutions:

- **Use Open Standards:** Frameworks like **ONNX Runtime and OpenVINO** enable AI models to run on multiple hardware platforms.

- **Adopt Unified AI Deployment Tools:** Tools like **TensorFlow Lite and PyTorch Mobile** simplify model deployment across edge devices.

- **Develop Cross-Platform APIs:** Middleware solutions allow different edge devices to communicate effectively.

☐ **Example:** The **Open Neural Network Exchange (ONNX)** enables AI models to be transferred between different frameworks and devices.

7.3 AI Ethics and Regulatory Concerns

Deploying AI at the edge raises serious **privacy, security, and ethical concerns**. Unlike cloud AI, where data processing occurs in secure data centers, Edge AI often handles **sensitive data** locally on personal or industrial devices.

Challenges:

Data Privacy Risks: Edge AI devices collect and process user data (e.g., smart home cameras, wearables), raising concerns about **data ownership** and **misuse**.

Security Threats: Edge devices are **vulnerable to hacking**, leading to potential **data breaches** or **AI manipulation**.

Bias in AI Models: AI models trained on **biased datasets** can result in unfair or inaccurate decisions.

Regulatory Compliance: Edge AI must comply with laws like **GDPR (Europe), CCPA (California), and AI Act (EU)**.

Solutions:

- **On-Device Encryption:** Encrypt sensitive data before processing or transmitting it.
- **Federated Learning:** Train AI models locally on edge devices without sharing raw data with the cloud.
- **Bias Detection & Fairness Audits:** Regularly audit AI models to detect and eliminate biases.
- **Regulatory Compliance Frameworks:** Follow

industry standards and privacy laws for ethical AI deployment.

☐ **Example:** Google's **federated learning** allows AI models on smartphones to **learn from user data locally** without sending raw data to the cloud, improving privacy.

7.4 The Future of AI on Edge Devices

The future of Edge AI is **promising**, with advancements in **hardware, software, and AI algorithms** making edge computing more powerful and efficient.

Key Trends Shaping the Future of Edge AI:

AI-Optimized Edge Hardware

Next-generation **AI chips and accelerators** will enable more complex models to run on edge devices. **Neuromorphic computing** (brain-inspired AI) will enhance efficiency in **real-time Edge AI processing**. **Battery-free AI** powered by energy harvesting will enable long-term AI operations in remote locations.

5G and Edge AI Synergy

5G networks will enable ultra-fast communication between edge devices and the cloud. **AI inference at the network edge** (MEC – Multi-Access Edge Computing) will enhance **real-time processing** for applications like **autonomous driving** and **smart factories**.

Decentralized and Collaborative AI

Swarm AI: Groups of edge devices (e.g., drones, robots) will **collaborate** to make decisions in real-time. **Blockchain for Edge AI:** Secure, decentralized AI models will allow **trustless AI collaborations** across devices.

4⬚Advanced AI Algorithms for Edge Computing

TinyML will drive AI into ultra-low-power devices, making **AI-powered IoT sensors** more intelligent. **Self-learning edge AI models** will **adapt to changing environments** without cloud retraining. **AI for Sustainability:** Energy-efficient AI models will power **climate monitoring, precision agriculture, and smart grids**.

Conclusion

While Edge AI presents unique challenges in **power efficiency, standardization, security, and ethical AI**, continuous innovations in **AI hardware, software, and connectivity** are overcoming these barriers.

Challenge	Solution	Future Trends
Power & Resource Constraints	Model compression, AI accelerators, TinyML	Neuromorphic computing, ultra-efficient AI
Standardization Issues	ONNX, OpenVINO, cross-platform tools	Unified AI deployment frameworks
AI Ethics & Privacy Risks	Federated learning, encryption, bias audits	Decentralized AI, blockchain for AI security

Limited Edge AI Capabilities	Efficient AI models, hardware optimizations	Self-learning AI, AI-powered 5G edge networks

Edge AI is **revolutionizing industries**, from **smart cities and autonomous vehicles** to **healthcare and retail**. As technology advances, **AI at the edge will become faster, smarter, and more energy-efficient**, unlocking new possibilities for real-time, privacy-preserving AI applications.

Chapter 8: Edge AI Best Practices

Successfully deploying **Edge AI** requires a strategic approach to **hardware selection, model optimization, security, and integration** with existing systems. This chapter provides practical guidelines for ensuring **efficient, secure, and scalable** Edge AI deployments.

8.1 Choosing the Right Hardware and Software Stack

Selecting the right **Edge AI hardware and software** depends on factors like **computational power, energy efficiency, cost, and deployment environment**.

Hardware Selection

- **Low-power microcontrollers** (e.g., Arduino, ESP32) → Ideal for TinyML applications in IoT sensors.
- **Single-board computers** (e.g., Raspberry Pi, NVIDIA Jetson Nano) → Suitable for lightweight AI inference.
- **AI accelerators** (e.g., Google Coral TPU, Intel Movidius) → Boosts AI model performance on edge devices.
- **FPGAs** (Field-Programmable Gate Arrays) → Customizable for high-speed AI processing.
- **Edge AI servers** (e.g., NVIDIA Jetson AGX, Intel Edge AI devices) → For high-performance industrial AI applications.

Software and AI Frameworks

Selecting the right AI framework ensures efficient deployment:

TensorFlow Lite → Optimized for mobile and embedded devices.

ONNX Runtime → Cross-platform compatibility for AI models.

OpenVINO → Optimized for Intel hardware and computer vision tasks.

PyTorch Mobile → Ideal for mobile and edge AI applications.

TinyML → Designed for ultra-low-power AI applications.

☐ **Example:** A security camera system may use **NVIDIA Jetson Xavier** with **TensorRT** for real-time **facial recognition** while maintaining power efficiency.

8.2 Optimizing Models for Efficiency

Deploying AI at the edge requires **efficient models** that run on limited hardware without sacrificing accuracy.

Optimization Techniques

- **Model Quantization** → Reduces model size by converting 32-bit floating-point weights into 8-bit integers, improving speed and reducing memory usage.
- **Model Pruning** → Removes **redundant neurons and connections**, making AI models lighter and faster.
- **Knowledge Distillation** → Trains a **smaller AI model** to mimic a larger, more complex one, maintaining accuracy while reducing size.
- **Edge-Specific Model Architectures** → Use **lightweight models** like MobileNet, EfficientNet, or YOLOv5 for real-time AI inference.

☐ **Example:** MobileNetV2 is **70% smaller** than traditional CNN models but performs well in **image classification tasks** on Edge AI devices.

Efficient Model Deployment

Use hardware acceleration → Enable GPU/TPU optimizations where possible.

Optimize inference time → Use tools like TensorFlow Lite's **Post-Training Optimization Toolkit**.

Reduce power consumption → Implement **adaptive AI models** that adjust processing power based on task complexity.

☐ **Example:** Smart home assistants **lower AI processing power** when in standby mode to conserve energy.

8.3 Security Considerations for Edge AI Deployment

Since Edge AI operates **outside centralized cloud environments**, it is **more vulnerable** to security threats.

Key Security Challenges:

Data privacy risks → Edge AI collects sensitive data that could be exposed if compromised.
Device tampering → Physical access to edge devices increases the risk of hacking.
Adversarial attacks → AI models can be manipulated using deceptive inputs.
Network vulnerabilities → Edge devices

communicating over **Wi-Fi, 5G, or IoT networks** are targets for cyberattacks.

Best Practices for Securing Edge AI

Secure boot and firmware updates → Ensure only authenticated firmware runs on edge devices. **On-device encryption** → Encrypt data both **at rest** and **in transit** to prevent unauthorized access. **Federated learning** → Train AI models **locally on devices** instead of transmitting raw data to the cloud. **Zero-trust security model** → Apply strict access control and authentication for all edge devices. **AI model watermarking** → Protect AI models from tampering and unauthorized use.

☐ **Example:** Tesla's **Autopilot AI models** use encrypted updates to prevent adversarial attacks on self-driving systems.

8.4 Integrating Edge AI with Existing Infrastructure

For Edge AI to be **useful at scale**, it must seamlessly integrate with **cloud computing, IoT devices, and enterprise systems**.

Integration Strategies

- **Hybrid AI Deployment** → Use **Edge AI** for real-time inference and send critical data to the **cloud for further analysis**.
- **Edge-to-Cloud Connectivity** → Implement **5G, LPWAN, or Wi-Fi** for secure data transfer between edge devices and cloud servers.
- **Interoperability with IoT Platforms** → Ensure Edge AI solutions work with **existing IoT ecosystems** like AWS IoT Greengrass, Google Cloud IoT, or Azure IoT Edge.
- **Containerized AI Deployment** → Use **Docker, Kubernetes, or EdgeX Foundry** for flexible deployment across multiple edge devices.
- **Remote Monitoring and Management** → Implement AI-powered dashboards to **monitor edge devices in real time**.

☐ **Example:** A **smart factory** can use Edge AI to detect equipment failures in real time, while **cloud analytics** optimize production efficiency.

Conclusion

Deploying **Edge AI** successfully requires careful **hardware selection, model optimization, security enhancements, and seamless integration** with existing infrastructures.

Best Practice	Key Takeaways
Choosing the Right Hardware	Match edge hardware to the AI task (low-power MCUs, AI accelerators, or industrial edge servers).
Selecting an AI Framework	Use **TensorFlow Lite, OpenVINO, ONNX Runtime, or PyTorch Mobile** for optimized edge AI inference.
Optimizing Models	Apply **quantization, pruning, and knowledge distillation** to reduce model size and latency.
Security Considerations	Implement **secure boot, encryption, federated learning, and AI model watermarking**.

Edge AI & Cloud Integration	Use **Edge-to-Cloud connectivity, hybrid AI deployment, and containerized AI** for scalability.

By following these **best practices**, businesses can deploy **scalable, efficient, and secure** Edge AI solutions that deliver **real-time intelligence** while preserving **privacy and cost efficiency**.

Conclusion

Edge AI is revolutionizing how **artificial intelligence** is deployed, bringing real-time decision-making directly to devices **without relying on cloud processing**. By enabling **low-latency, secure, and efficient AI** at the edge, businesses and developers can create smarter, faster, and more **cost-effective AI-powered solutions**.

Key Takeaways

Edge AI reduces latency by processing data locally, enabling real-time decision-making for **autonomous vehicles, industrial automation, and smart surveillance**.

Security and privacy are enhanced since sensitive data is processed on the device, reducing risks associated with cloud-based AI.

Lower cloud dependency leads to cost savings, especially in industries requiring large-scale AI deployments.

Edge AI is scalable and energy-efficient, making it ideal for IoT, TinyML applications, and AI-driven smart cities.

Successful Edge AI implementation requires **careful hardware selection, model optimization, security measures, and seamless integration with existing infrastructures**.

The Future of Edge AI

As AI hardware and software continue to **evolve**, Edge AI will become even **more powerful, efficient, and widespread**. Key trends shaping the future include:

- **5G-powered Edge AI** → Faster connectivity for real-time AI processing in smart cities and industrial IoT.
- **AI model efficiency improvements** → Advances in **quantization, pruning, and knowledge distillation** will enable even **smaller, more efficient AI models**.
- **More robust Edge AI security frameworks** → As adoption grows, new security measures will protect AI models and data from cyber threats.
- **Increased adoption across industries** → From **healthcare** to **retail**, Edge AI will drive **next-generation automation and decision-making**.

By leveraging **Edge AI's potential**, businesses can **unlock new opportunities, enhance operational efficiency, and build AI-driven solutions that are faster, smarter, and more sustainable**.

Table of Contents

www.ingramcontent.com/pod-product-compliance
Lightning Source LLC
LaVergne TN
LVHW051540050326
832903LV00033B/4356